Copyright © 2015 by M.E. Porter
All rights reserved.
ISBN: 1945117079
ISBN-13: 978-1945117077

Library of Congress Control Number: 2016939331

The Pieces of ME

The Pieces OF ME

(AND YOU)

When all is well in my Soul; all is well in the world.

The Pieces of ME

An Autobiographical Journal

These pieces belong to:

_____

I am dedicated to my own growth and healing process, therefore I am committed to doing the work required within the pages of this book. I am committed to finding the pieces of me.

DEDICATION

This book is dedicated to my children:

Misha, the first-born and my biggest cheerleader;

Christina, the feisty, eclectic middle child –

I am her secret super hero;

and

Charity, the baby girl and The Mini-ME.

I thank God for allowing these souls to be entrusted to ME.

I love you three ladies to life and am honored to be your Mommy!

When all is well in my Soul; all is well in the world.

FOREWORD

"M. E. Porter - The Soul Shifter - is a beacon of light to all those who are seeking to find their SOULself. Her ability to be transparent and give of herself completely in order to facilitate transformation in all those she comes in contact with is experienced at a deeper level in her new work: ***The Pieces of ME***! As you read the pages of this book, I challenge you to see yourself in her words and see the light at the end of the tunnel we have each created for ourselves. You will be enlightened and empowered - and she shall truly speak to your soul with the words within this work!"

Famira M. Green, Branding Guru & Visual Impactologist

When all is well in my Soul; all is well in the world.

1

NEATLY SCATTERED

Behold, I was shapen in iniquity;

and in sin did my mother conceive me.

Psalm 51:5

My story is just that: my story. It's not intended to cast a shadow on the trials and mishaps of anyone else's story, but merely serves as an opportunity for me to share a few pieces of myself with the world. Statistically speaking, M.E. Porter's story will not differ much from most African American females born in the late 60's to unwed, uneducated, poverty-stricken mothers.

Statistics is the science of numerical data, and the numbers don't lie. I breeched the earth's atmosphere straight into the Royal Court of Negative Statistics: poor, black, fatherless, and female - which doesn't look so bad if you consider I was never supposed to be here anyway. But God!

In 1966, doctors put my mother's mangled body back together after a near-fatal car wreck. Of the five people in the vehicle, my mother was the only one ejected – through the floorboard of the car – which left her internally irreparable. I, Marilyn Elizabeth, arrived three years later in November 1969: **GOD IS GOOD!**

When all is well in my Soul; all is well in the world.

I am predestined to defy the odds. My very presence here is a direct blow to the enemy who desired to destroy my mother's womb in a frantic effort to silence the anointing God would have on my life. How many of you know that an anointed life does **not** equate to a life without struggle, mistakes, regrets, uncertainty, and (oftentimes) utter turmoil? Thus, my reign in the Royal Court of Negative Statistics did not end at birth.

I did have one exceptional advantage that afforded me the courage to think, dream, and believe myself to be worthy of more than *the hood* had to offer: I was blessed with a gift of God-given wisdom **and** a high natural intellect. Simply put, I was *the smart girl*. Those around me often made attempts to secretly belittle my intellect. I was exposed to jokes on a daily basis by family members and neighbors. I recall one of my cousins – who profoundly begrudged me because her mother regularly compared her academic abilities to mine – always laughing and pointing her finger at me saying, "It's not anybody's fault that you were already potty-trained when you came out of the womb!" Her intention was to make me feel awkward and weirdly, overly more mature than all of the other children - but I never felt that. On the contrary, I was always thankful that I was not as silly-acting and unlearned as those around me – even the adults.

My mother parented me to the best of her meager 8th grade education - and would proudly and unashamedly tell anyone that by the time I was five years old, she knew that I was already far more intelligent than she. I would hear her tell my aunts and her closest friends, *"I didn't really know what to do with her. Before she even started kindergarten, she was already smarter than me. I knew that all I could offer her in life would be to provide her with food, clothing, and shelter. I would never be able to teach her anything of great value, so I just loved her and protected her to the best of my abilities."*

My mother was all I had in the world, and I thought her to be a hero. I don't believe I ever realized that I was more intelligent than she; however, I recall being *un-parented* – which, as a child, translates as *unloved*. My mother was not a *bad* mother. In my heart of hearts, I believe she gave me the very best pieces of herself – but as the princess of the Royal Court of Negative Statistics, her efforts

When all is well in my Soul; all is well in the world.

to protect me fell short on many occasions throughout my childhood.

(I have never faulted my mother for her fails. After all, it should have been my father standing strongly in that role of protector.)

The Pieces of YOU:

When all is well in my Soul; all is well in the world.

The Pieces of ME

I was born late in the year of 1969 - a November baby - which made me ineligible to start school at the exact age of five. I was nearly six when I began my public school education – but that is neither here nor there to the subject matter of my mother's desire to educate her own self for the sake of me. In the Summer before I entered Kindergarten, my mother made a bold decision to enter into our local community college's Adult Education program, which would allow her to simultaneously earn her high school diploma and college credits (this had no real meaning or value to me, but she seemed happy, thus - I was happy for her.)

Mother would leave the house very early on certain days (memory does not permit me to recall the exact days of the week, but I clearly remember that on those days, I had to prepare my own breakfast and myself before I walked to the neighbor's to be babysat). It's quite funny now as I think about it: It would seem that a child with the ability to dress oneself, feed oneself, and deliver oneself to the babysitter - did not need a babysitter! One particular day – and what a day it turned out to be – my mother decided that a

When all is well in my Soul; all is well in the world.

gentleman she had been dating for some time was trustworthy enough to remain in the house with me to serve as my sitter.

Even as a child, I was very consistent in my way and I *consistently* had to have my two Chips-Ahoy chocolate chip cookies – the ones in the blue bag (in my day, we did not have the plethora of varieties you can buy today) – as my afternoon snack. This day was no different – not concerning my need for those cookies, anyway. I recall running into the house and heading straight for the kitchen. No one had to tell me where my cookies were and no one had to serve them to me…but when I entered the kitchen, there *he* stood, smiling at me and holding the bag of cookies in his giant hands. I remember thinking, "What is he doing with those cookies? Doesn't he know that no one is supposed to touch those except me?"

Perhaps the rant of an only child, I was certainly not accustomed to sharing my Chips-Ahoy! Yet, there he stood with his eyes piercing right through me with those cookies far too high in the air for me to reach them. After a brief staring match, he finally spoke: "You want your afternoon snack?" It felt creepy to me, almost as if he had asked me a trick question – one that no matter how I replied would leave me doomed. "Yes please," I replied in my quiet 5-year-old toned voice. "Ok, then come over here and touch *this!*" He pointed to his still-clothed – but hard – penis. Admittedly, I didn't have a vast understanding of just what a penis was, but I knew it was the thing that made me different from my best buddy who lived next door, and he was a boy.

I remember the fear of that moment. You see, just a few weeks earlier, my neighbor and I had been playing in the front yard on a lounge chair and we covered ourselves with a wool blanket in an attempt to create a fort. Well, when his grandmother looked outside, she yelled, "You all get from under that blanket right now!" She summoned him into the house and sent me home. It was quite confusing, but I was smart enough to figure out it had something to do with the fact that I was a girl and he was a boy – after all, this didn't happen when I made forts with my girl neighbors.

Back to *him*. So, I had an understanding that as a girl, I should not be touching a boy – especially not one this big. I gathered myself, jumped up, grabbed the bag, and ran out of the house.

When all is well in my Soul; all is well in the world.

Thinking that I had escaped his foolery, I saw no need to tell my mother of this incident – but I could not have been more wrong.

The Pieces of YOU:

When all is well in my Soul; all is well in the world.

The Pieces of ME

There are events that shape who we are, who we become, and who we think ourselves to be deep in the depths of our hearts, and that moment of fear standing in my mother's kitchen had stolen my innocence: the world no longer felt safe, I no longer felt free, and on that day, I ceased to be a child. I no longer desired my Chips-Ahoy cookies or anything that made me feel the freedoms of childhood.

My mother continued to pursue her GED and she continued to date this gentleman as well, but something changed: she began to send me away on the weekends that he would come to our home and he didn't spend the night during the week. I wondered if she knew what had happened between us (in my mind *he* had not done something wrong…*we* had done something wrong. I thought myself to be as guilty as he). Then it happened.

My mother was late for school on what had to be a Monday because I had spent the weekend at my Aunt's house. When I was dropped off at home that morning, *he* was still there and my mom said those fatal words: "You can just stay here with him today. Don't go to the sitter!" and she hurried out the door. I was terrified! As the

When all is well in my Soul; all is well in the world.

day went on, I became sick and my mom came home to care for me, but he stayed under the guise of helping her.

Later that night, perhaps in the wee hours of the morning, I woke to the sound of my mother weeping. It wasn't really a cry. Neither did it sound as if she was in pain. It was almost a whimper. As an adult, I now understand that the sound was generated through an act of intimacy with her gentleman. I laid there listening until I no longer heard the sound of my mother's whimper, and as I turned to go back to sleep, I felt a hand on my back. I knew that it was not my mom. I knew her touch. I was familiar with the size her hand and even her breathing pattern. This was a giant hand - the one I saw grip my Chips-Ahoy just a few months prior.

Now, many would say that the gentleman molested me, but not me. No. I am going to call a spade a spade: He RAPED me. In that moment, my limited 5-year-old understanding didn't quite know what was happening to me - only that it was happening and that it was causing me pain.

Journal Work: This book was written and designed to not only be thought-provoking, but to be emotionally-cleansing. STOP. Consider the things *you* have experienced in your younger life that may have had a violent impact. After you read the next section, there will be lines provided for you to express yourself.

When all is well in my Soul; all is well in the world.

The Innocence Thief

Allow ME to take this opportunity to talk to the parents (and those who will be parents someday). Fathers, Mothers, Grandparents, Aunts, Uncles, Cousins, Step and Foster parents, please know how important it is for a child to feel safe to be a child. Childhood is a very necessary part of the human experience. It shapes the outcome of our adolescence and, subsequently, our adult lives.

"Innocence stolen is childhood stolen."

~ M.E. Porter.

As you can see from my story, the innocence was stolen before the physical violation of my body occurred. Innocence was stolen in the moments when fear, guilt and condemnation set in. Protect your children from exposure to the following adjectives: hurtful, secretive, mysterious, horrified, guilty, and angry – things that cause them to surrender their innocence. Protect your children's innocence as if their very lives depend on it - because their lives **do** depend on it.

The Pieces of YOU:

When all is well in my Soul; all is well in the world.

The Pieces of ME

When all is well in my Soul; all is well in the world.

This is an emotional journey to travel, but I have found that others tend to be far more uncomfortable with my story than I. I have watched the looks of terror come across women's faces at times when I have shared these pieces of me. I've felt the temperature of the room change as tears form in the corners of the eyes of those under the sound my voice – and understandably so. Rape is a devastatingly horrid act, but the rape of a *child* causes a lump to rise in one's throat. It is a difficult story to swallow.

Knowing that God alone has given me the strength to recall these pieces of me and tell of them with ease causes me to praise Him outrageously! The Bible tells us that there is a time and a season to everything - and to this add that there is also a ***purpose***. *A purpose?* Surely, this woman cannot believe that there was a ***purpose*** in being raped! Is she crazy? NO, beloved: I am not crazy. I am simply a Believer of God and His Word: *"And we know that in all things God works for the good of those who love Him, and are called according to His purpose."* (Romans 8:28) I know that I am called to His purpose, therefore everything in the Royal Court of Negative Statistics must work in my favor!

M.E. SPEAKS: A sexually-improper touch, inappropriate sexual language, or a visual introduction to sexually-explicit actions or imagery – these are acts that can be labeled as *molestation*. Penetration of any kind (anal or vaginal) with any object or body part, oral engagement of any kind (mouth-to-mouth or mouth to penis or vagina) – these are acts that can be labeled as *rape*. Know that the moment a child is put in any sexually-uncomfortable situation by anyone, their soul retains that information and it will respond to that negative impact someday, somehow, in some way.

When tragic events shape your beginnings, it is easy to allow those events to define who you are. Somehow, I never did. As a teenager, I was not star-struck. In fact, I believed the celebrities would have done well to meet ME more than me being obsessed with meeting them. This was not haughty thinking, but I had a sense of my God-ordained value. I understood how completely special I was to God and that out of the millions of sperm cells that had raced to penetrate the egg in my mother's womb, God had declared ME the winner!

When all is well in my Soul; all is well in the world.

I have been asked on many occasions how did I understand and trust the love of God so thoroughly at such a young age. You see, we must go back to the night my mother's boyfriend entered my bedroom just a few short moments after he had laid with her. I saw an angel in my bedroom. I was too young to be afraid - plus there was such a calm in me that even the fear I had originally felt had dissipated. My eyes had been shut tight during the violation, but when I opened them, there was a man standing in my bedroom near my dresser. It was the silhouette of a man (there was no substance to him, yet I could clearly see him weeping as he watched this man ravage my body).

When my mother's gentleman was done, he looked down at me with horrific regret in his eyes as if he had come to his senses and realized that I would more than likely tell my mother of his actions as soon as the opportunity presented itself. He removed the pillow from under my head and stood there for a moment in total silence – I remained unafraid with my eyes fixated on the silhouette standing near my dresser…it had begun to move closer to my bed.

Suddenly, it was over. My rapist dropped the pillow and left my room. The silhouette – my angel – was gone.

When all is well in my Soul; all is well in the world.

Journal Work: Take this moment to sit and reflect with your own experiences. Recall the moments in your young life when you may have been faced with feeling helpless and afraid. Can you recall if there was anyone you felt should have been there to comfort you? Are you holding on to the fears and anxieties of that moment?

The Pieces of YOU:

_____

_____

_____

_____

_____

_____

_____

_____

_____

_____

_____

_____

When all is well in my Soul; all is well in the world.

The Pieces of ME

When all is well in my Soul; all is well in the world.

As a child, I didn't know the words to explain what I had witnessed. God had sent an angel - an angel of *mercy* - and because of that mercy, that night my life was spared. Thinking back, I am certain that the rapist desired to kill me that night, but God's love and protection kept me. How do I know my value, you may ask? How do I know that I am a divine design? How do I know that every aspect of my living has been ordained, precisely chosen, and approved by God in His infinite wisdom? Because He has sustained me. He brought me to this place called earth against the doctor's report. He kept me drug-free and alcohol-free amid nearly everyone in my life being consumed and overtaken by substance abuse. He sustained me through being taunted and bullied. After the story of my rape became public knowledge, the children in my neighborhood would refer to me as "the girl who did the nasty with her mom's boyfriend". That alone is enough to cause one to develop some habits - but He sustained me. For these reasons, I will not die without fulfilling the call on my life. I will not die with my purpose for being here left unlived. I shall be all that God has orchestrated for me to be in my time.

The Pieces of YOU:

When all is well in my Soul; all is well in the world.

The Pieces of ME

When all is well in my Soul; all is well in the world.

2

EYES WIDE SHUT

"The beginning of wisdom is: Acquire wisdom;

And with all your acquiring, get understanding.

Proverbs 4:7

The road to triumph can be a lonely one and I know there are so many others who could tell a similar story; however, there is no one that can tell of M.E.'s "experience". I often did not know that I was having a tragic existence.

I didn't know that being an 18-year-old bride with only a high school diploma in my hand and no real plan to survive in the world, other than my very low-ranking military husband – who was only 19 himself - was tragic.

I had grown up a welfare kid in a poverty-stricken neighborhood smack dab in the middle of suburbia, and my closest friends and confidants were drug dealers, junkies, and prostitutes. (Just writing that sentence calls to my mind "Amazing Grace" – He truly saved a wretch like ME.)

I didn't know that losing six babies to miscarriages was tragic because I was so emotionally-stunted that I had no connection to those blessings in my womb.

When all is well in my Soul; all is well in the world.

I didn't know that coming home and finding another woman's panties hidden in my couch cushions was tragic, because at least my couch was in a house that was not in *"the hood"*.

I didn't know that while separated from my husband and becoming impregnated with another man's child was tragic, because at least the other man wasn't my cousin or my uncle – which had been the norm in my family (the pregnancy, by the way, ended in an abortion – which I also did not know was tragic, because in my neighborhood it was merely a form of birth control).

I didn't know it was tragic when I became pregnant with my second child - freshly-divorced from husband number one - and found myself with no means of caring for the child I already had nor for the one in my womb.

The Pieces of YOU:

_____
_____
_____
_____
_____
_____
_____
_____
_____
_____
_____
_____
_____
_____
_____
_____
_____
_____
_____
_____
_____

When all is well in my Soul; all is well in the world.

The Pieces of ME

When all is well in my Soul; all is well in the world.

What I **did** know was how to manipulate (I had learned that early on in life). So, I simply cried to the unborn child's father who, by the way, had made it clear that he did not have *any* desire to be married or have *any* more children (years later we would find out that the children he thought were his prior to my pregnancy were not his – yet another tragedy). He succumbed to my tears, and we married while I was just nine weeks pregnant. Marriage was the solution to healthcare and housing, but it did not increase my value. It was, in fact, one of the most dishonoring and devaluing experiences I have encountered thus far.

Journal Work: Again, I urge you to take these moments to truly search the depths of who you are and why you are who you are. *DO THE WORK.* Don't leave these pages blank. Fill them with thoughts and words that could very well prepare and release you into the greatness of your life. Consider the following thought as you read the next section:

Single does not mean alone.

Don't Dishonor Yourself

I digress for just a moment to speak to the singles. Yes, beloveds. You read correctly. He **told** me that he did not want to be married. It was not a personal thing. It wasn't that he didn't want to marry *me*; he simply did not believe in the institution of marriage. Let me repeat it again: "**He told me that he did not want to be married.**" I didn't believe him. I believed I was the game-changer and he would marry me sooner or later. I beg of you beloveds: Do not take this path! The late, great Maya Angelou left us with this great and profound wisdom: *"When a person tells you who they are, believe*

When all is well in my Soul; all is well in the world.

them." Yes, there is a time to allow some to grow and mature, but not at the expense of compromising all of your **own** values.

I tell my friends and clients the following words from the mouth of M.E. Porter:

> ***"Loyalty to another does not require disloyalty to self."***

He did not require this of me, but I attached my sense of loyalty to someone who was not only **not** deserving of it, but also didn't require or **ask** for it. He told me the following words after six months of dating: "I love you, but I will never want to marry you. If we are together 30 years from now, I will not want to marry you." Singles: When he/she tells you who they are, ***believe them***! He told me by default that he was not marriage material. Is someone telling you the same thing?

The Pieces of YOU:

When all is well in my Soul; all is well in the world.

The Pieces of ME

When all is well in my Soul; all is well in the world.

The Pieces of ME

So, it was about this time - at the age of 27 - that I began to recognize the "TRA" in my tragic life, while yet racking up continuous statistical data in the Royal Court. *My data now included: divorce, being an unwanted and unloved wife, a college dropout, and I was buried in debt.* I was feeling the tremendous pain of being married yet single, but since he took care of me and my daughters, I remained in the sad, lonely, depressing, civilly-united partnership disguised as marriage (after all, I had become the "Mistress of Disguise"). Even in the throes of this misery, I had yet to recognize the "GEDY" of tragedy I was amid. But God!

It was in this place that my emotions that had been halted at five years old began to come alive - and it was nearly unbearable. I realized that to hear God the way I needed to, I had to *feel* Him - and I desperately wanted to hear God. So, I allowed myself to feel. Allow ME to share the words with you that will perhaps describe the flood of emotions that flooded my very being:

When all is well in my Soul; all is well in the world.

"Oh my God: he raped me! Where was my daddy? Why did he let that happen to me?"

"I heard my parents on the phone. I heard my father tell my mother that he does not love me."

"I hated being teased for living in 'The Hole in The Wall'."

"I hated using those bright pink tickets in the lunchroom at school. It told everyone that I got free lunch and was a welfare kid."

"My mom didn't buy me toothbrushes or do my laundry as a child, and I always got picked on for stinking."

"I don't want to have sex with this boy, but how can I say no – I don't know how to say no. God please do something."

"My mom gossips about me with her friends. Their daughters come back and tell me things that only she would know. I don't have anyone in the world I can trust."

"I won't go to college after all. It's too much of a risk. My whole family is counting on me to succeed. I am too afraid of failing."

"I never told him that I found that woman's panties between the cushions of the couch in my house!"

"I saw my husband look at me and turn up his nose as if I was nasty to him while were having sex."

"Will God forgive me for aborting my child? I still remember his/her birthday: December 10, 1995."

"God, please help me not to hate him for leaving me and my children alone. They lay by the door at night with their pillows waiting for him to come home. PLEASE God: I don't want to hate him!"

Can you just imagine the emotion attached to those words?

When all is well in my Soul; all is well in the world.

The Pieces of ME

The Pieces of YOU:

When all is well in my Soul; all is well in the world.

The Pieces of ME

At times, I would feel the pain so deeply that I would not be able to stand. I would simply fall to the floor and weep. The pain rendered me weak, but in my weakness, God was right there. I was no longer ignoring the issues or holding back the tears that had been trying to fall from my eyes for so long. In this state of brokenness, God began to speak clearly to my heart. In this broken state of being, He began to give the vision for His will in my life: I was to serve Him by serving His daughters. My living had not been in vain. The pain of my tragic existence (yes, I saw it all now - the entire T-R-A-G-E-D & Y!) and the numerical data I had been gathering in the Royal Court of Negative Statistics had merely been that He might get the glory of my story in the end. So, I glorify Him in **all** things and I thank Him for every trial, every lesson, and every outcome.

Even in the midst of the mess, God will show a glimpse of His glory. I know there were many times when I could see the possibilities of God using me for something great (greatness is relative and cannot be compared among individuals). In 1998, I began to feel a tug at my heart towards ministry. I had begun to study the Word of God extensively while I was pregnant with my

When all is well in my Soul; all is well in the world.

second child, so although I had acquired an understanding of what it meant to serve the people of God, the turmoil of my personal life at the time still would not allow me to fully embrace the notion of ME being a chosen vessel to preach and teach The Gospel. Thanks be unto God that He will always confirm Himself and make the path clear, and this is exactly what He began to do - through other anointed women and men of God.

M.E. SPEAKS: I have said so much in this chapter. So much emotion, so much pain. Please don't move onto the final piece without giving yourself a much-deserved opportunity to visit your own emotions - especially those that may be yet attached to things of the past. Here, I offer you the opportunity to also share with M.E. Yes, I'd like for you to send M.E. an email of your journaling exercises. Send it to theemotionalme@marilyneporter.com .

The Pieces of YOU:

When all is well in my Soul; all is well in the world.

The Pieces of ME

When all is well in my Soul; all is well in the world.

3

MANIFESTING LIGHT

"I am a guiding light; I shine light into dark places"

The vision began to seep into my soul while my 'then husband' was stationed at Bolling AFB, Washington DC where I became involved with the PWOC (Protestant Women of The Chapel) and realized that I had a gift of wisdom. Other women clung to that wisdom as a means of helping them get through their own trials. I quickly became the president of the organization and well-known as a leader of women. It was in this move of God that I began to reflect back on my childhood and retrieve memories of myself as a child being the leader among all of the girls in my neighborhood. I was always teaching them something - from how to sew a button on a dress or cooking to memorizing the 23rd Psalm. Each passing day, I felt myself become more open to the truth of my calling and soon, just a few short months before my 30th birthday, I accepted that I was certainly purposed for the path of ministry: more specifically, women's ministry. (God has sense of humor, because women had not been my favorite people!)

A glimpse of the vision to an immature and slightly disobedient child can be damaging in ministry because in your zeal and immaturity, you think that it is the fullness of the vision – while

When all is well in my Soul; all is well in the world.

there are yet many more pieces to be revealed. I, like others before me (and I am sure others that are yet to come), became so excited with the vision that I moved ahead of God's plan. With no training, _church affiliation, or spiritual leadership of any kind, I began *ARISE! Ministries – Ministry for Women by Women.* ARISE! was received with open arms by all those around me, but to others it was deemed a rogue ministry. Women were blessed during our conferences and meetings. The ministry received outside financial support (held IRS 501(c) (3) status) and was also sustained by tithes and offerings, but that was not enough to sustain my character – and after roughly two years in operation, ARISE! Ministries was no more. I had been disobedient and because of that disobedience, God silenced my voice in ministry in November 2003.

Journal Work: It's tough to have a great idea burning in your belly and not act on it. I know this all too well; however, many times when we receive the vision, it is merely a means of letting us know that we are worthy to be given a vision and not actually the moment to execute. Have there been times in your life that you have moved too soon and things just didn't work out? Are you in that space right now? Honesty is the key, so please take a moment and get truly authentic with yourself about your vision. Is it a right-now vision or could you use someone to come alongside you and offer you answers and support? **BE HONEST** and let go of the notion that you can do it all by yourself!

When all is well in my Soul; all is well in the world.

The Pieces of YOU:

When all is well in my Soul; all is well in the world.

The Pieces of ME

I often felt like Moses on the back side of the desert during the years between 2003 and 2013. Ten years is a long time to be silenced while the vision is yet clear in your mind, heart, and spirit. There were years of doubting, pouting, and being angry with God for giving me a glimpse of the vision and then taking away my permissions to operate in or towards the vision. Don't get me wrong: I was allowed moments in which I could minister. I have always been wise and He always permitted me to give wise counsel to those who sought it. He would always permit me to assist others in establishing their ministry organizations – paperwork mostly, but nonetheless they were opportunities for me to use some of the gifts inside of me. Then, just when I had made peace with the idea that perhaps my ministry had become one that would encompass simply assisting others in fulfilling *their* visions, God spoke and breathed the breath of life back into my whole-hearted desire to bring healing to my sisters all over the world!

It was a Thursday morning in August 2013 when The Spirit spoke: "NOW, create a ministry for other women that is designed just as you are. Let your personality and demeanor speak to women.

When all is well in my Soul; all is well in the world.

Encourage them, teach them, and motivate them to seek me more." To God be the glory! From that instruction came "Motivationally ME" – the ministry of motivation.

Ten years!

Two divorces.

Three children.

Eight years to earn one college degree.

Ten addresses.

Hundreds of sleepless nights and…

Millions of prayers later – THE VISION IS YET ALIVE!

In this digital age, global ministry is not a difficult task, so I took to the Internet to honor my Father's instructions to go forth. I created a Facebook page on that same Thursday morning in August 2013. Like everyone else on the social media outlet, I began with one "LIKE" - and that was my own. I wasn't really concerned with the popularity of the page. I simply wanted to be obedient.

Motivationally ME (by design) represented my personality: energetic, jovial, praise-packed, and a lover of the Bible - and it carried my initials "M"arilyn "E"lizabeth while reflecting areas of God's character: love, support, kindness, gentle instruction, and wisdom.

When all is well in my Soul; all is well in the world.

Pieces of YOU

Question: What things has God instructed you to do a *specific* way?

When all is well in my Soul; all is well in the world.

The Pieces of ME

The Pieces of YOU

Write The Vision (Habakkuk 2:2):

When all is well in my Soul; all is well in the world.

The Pieces of ME

When all is well in my Soul; all is well in the world.

The Pieces of ME

The Pieces of YOU

Write the Instruction:

When all is well in my Soul; all is well in the world.

The Pieces of ME

I rested well that night with my one "LIKE" and a few others from some close and supportive friends. I was obediently happy, but I didn't know what was to come.

With a smile on my face and peace abounding in my heart, I rose on Friday morning eager to post some encouraging words on Motivationally ME. What I saw made me gasp for air. Overnight, the page had grown from about 10 "LIKES" to 3,000 fans! There was only about six posts on the page, but the people were flocking to Motivationally ME. Not only were they coming, but I already had messages in my inbox asking me if I had written books and, if so, how could they acquire a copy. I didn't quite know what I had done to draw the people, so I just wrote posts and shared pictures that spoke to ME. Throughout that Friday, roughly 800 to 900 more fans came to the page. I was thankful. When I awoke on Saturday morning, Motivationally ME had a whopping 7,500 fans! In less than 72 hours, I had become a Facebook notable and ministry was going forth in the entire United States **and** 30 countries! How great is our God?

When all is well in my Soul; all is well in the world.

Since its inception nearly two years ago now – I have invested so much of my time in the ministry that it seems as though it's been around for years – I have put a team of ladies in place (perhaps not so uniquely called "Team ME") to stand with me in service. I have been working on a teleconference series titled "HERSTORY" for about two years now, and it will be my prize project for Motivationally ME for 2014–15. Myself and 11 other ladies will pen a book and film a documentary to follow up the teleconference series. I hosted the "Spring to LIFE!" Virtual Event in May 2014 – an event that streamed live for 7 hours around the world on YouTube (that culminated the beginning of fulfilling a prophetic word that the ministry would have a global presence).

The Motivationally ME platform has opened up many opportunities for me as a businesswoman as well. Being of the sound, biblically-infused guidance and advice that I have given to my Facebook community, I have gained clients and now serve others not only in ministry, but as a life coach. In June of 2014, "Marilyn Elizabeth Unlimited LLC (The ME Brand)" became a legal entity – and is the parent company to several faith-based, personal development, coaching, and consulting programs. I also serve as a Spiritual Mentor and Spiritual Support Staff for several organizations. There is also a philanthropic component to ME Unlimited (yes, we must always give back): Charming ME© "Cultivating Class with Christ" – etiquette and image consulting for women between the ages of 16 and 24, where life skills and empowerment techniques are taught to affirm and confirm a young woman's awareness of self-love and self-respect.

I have been asked on many an occasion exactly how Motivationally ME gained such notoriety with such momentum, and my answer remains the same: Motivationally ME is simply a gift of my obedience from The Father. The ministry of Motivation – I don't know that I would have bought into it myself a few years ago, but God has used it so profoundly to serve and save His people. At the very beginning, when I first began the Thursday night "Motivation in Action" phone calls, a young lady called in and shared this testimony:

When all is well in my Soul; all is well in the world.

"I was sitting on my bed feeling low. I believe I have been in a depression for a long time - at least since I was hurt on the job a few years ago. I am constantly in pain and am tired of taking all of this medication all of the time. Quite frankly, I was on the verge of completely giving up. I had deleted my Facebook page, or at least I thought I had, and I am sitting here on my bed with all of my medications lined up before me. Just moments ago, I was preparing to take my own life and then my computer screen lit up and the Facebook page that I thought I had deleted popped up. On it was Motivationally ME, with an invitation for anyone who needed prayer to call in or chat live with you all. I KNOW that was God. I KNOW that this is not just a Facebook ministry. You are a real person who responds and interacts with people, and I am praising God for you and this ministry!"

The Pieces of YOU

Question: Whose life and/or destiny is waiting on you to follow the instructions that will bring your vision to life?

When all is well in my Soul; all is well in the world.

The Pieces of ME

When all is well in my Soul; all is well in the world.

I believe that woman's testimony says it all. The very name is designed to call you back to yourself. When you say "Motivationally ME", you are speaking encouragement back to yourself. Like the Psalmist David, we must sometimes encourage and motivate our **own** selves. Sometimes, I have to motivate me and there will be times when you have to motivate you, but when you can't find the strength to encourage yourself, God has ME positioned in a place that can offer encouragement 24 hours a day! Motivationally ME – *Keeping a smile on your face, placing a song on your heart, and motivation for your soul.*

While I am yet preparing to travel the world for the cause of Christ, you can find ME on Facebook serving up ministry to the masses every day. In 2014, I was honored with an award: **The 2014 Lady of Purpose Trailblazer Award**. *Purpose* – yes, my life has been divinely purposed in its entirety: the once fatherless, bullied, afraid, abused, unloved, unwanted, powerless, little bow-legged brown girl from a neighborhood that the town nicknamed "The Hole in the Wall." **All** of that was absolutely purposed! When I reflect back on all the days of my life, I feel such an overwhelming sense of joy and gratitude. The Creator of The Universe thought enough of ME to entrust ME with trials that may have broken most; yet, I have never experienced a moment where I felt the need to take a drink or have a smoke. I have always just had a little talk with Jesus to make it alright. I am a proud ambassador for Christ. That is who I am and that is what I do.

I have tossed and turned, cried and screamed - sometimes until my eyes were swollen and my voice eluded me.

I have told some lies and I have lived some.

I have hidden sin and hatred in my heart.

I have been an adulteress.

I have been a backstabber.

I have had my days of promiscuity.

I have been diminished, dishonored, devalued, driven to the edge, and just plain old dogged out… BUT DEAR GOD, I AM HERE! Thank you, Father, for carving out a path that no one else could walk.

When all is well in my Soul; all is well in the world.

With a brazen boldness, I stand at the ready to serve the world with the gift of stirring the souls of people. I am a Soul Shifter – I am designed to speak life and speak life and speak life - not just to your head and heart, but to your soul. It has been such an amazing path to becoming ME!

I am in love with **all** of *The Pieces of M.E.*

M.E.'s Life Gemstones

- ❖ Accountability means telling your truth 100% of the time so that another can enlightened.
- ❖ You can't make people respect you, but you don't have to stick around to be disrespected. You get to choose.
- ❖ God's instructions are not to make you perfect. They are a guideline so that you can know when you are getting off-track.
- ❖ "Maybe" is not an answer. It's your fear of saying "no".
- ❖ Your heart may lie to you and your spirit may be deceived, but your soul always knows the truth.
- ❖ God writes love poems and He titled mine Marilyn Elizabeth (insert YOUR name).

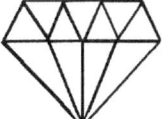 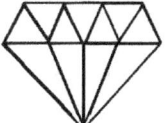 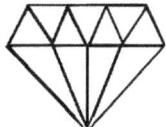

When all is well in my Soul; all is well in the world.

Who is M.E. Porter?

Woman.	Mother.	Minister.	Teacher.	Motivator.
Servant.	Friend.	Visionary.	Healer.	Trailblazer.
Author.	Speaker.	Coach.	Leader.	Believer.
Dreamer.	Entrepreneur.	Exhorter.	Edifier.	Encourager.

The Woman: I stand gracefully in the world as a woman called to a divine purpose. I am a Woman without regret about being a powerful and sensitive human being, and I have no desire to assume the role created for men.

The Mompreneur: I am the CEO and Founder of *Marilyn Elizabeth Unlimited, LLC (The ME Brand) – a faith-based coaching and personal development firm*. I help transform lives and lift women where they stand. Together, we stamp out chaos, confusion, and stagnation. The result is the alignment of words, actions, and spirit.

The Motivator: I am anointed to empower and propel others forward in their life journey. I assure my clients and business partners that our partnerships will never be steeped in mediocrity.

When clients work with me, they become undeniably aware of the incongruence in their lives and learn how to shift from strife to thrive. In the partnerships I form with my Sister-Clients, they learn to align their ***Do with their Who and Why***.

The Leader: Even as a child, other children were drawn to M.E. to lead the way. I was never afraid to step into the water first. I have always been willing to take the seat directly behind God and carry those behind me to the finish line. This aptitude has been an essential tool for my work with clients and organizations.

There is a thread of joy throughout my work. As a Spiritual Life Coach, it is made manifest in the lifting of clients' spirits so that they gain a level of self-efficacy, skills to effectively serve, and to lead others in a transformative manner based on biblical principles. As a Spiritual Life Coach and Speaker, I deliver God's word in church services, retreats, conferences, and secular leadership engagements.

The Author: As an author, I write about topics that will inspire people that seek liberation, empowerment, joy, and prosperity. In my work, I tell of His goodness and unfailing love in the darkest of circumstances in my life. I firmly believe that we should *"Trust in The Lord with all your heart and lean not on your understanding; in all your ways submit to him, and her will make your paths straight." Proverbs 3:5-6*

The Minister: In my work as a Minister, NO matter what the situation or circumstance, I will always give you a divine word. I may not give you scripture, but I will always give you Jesus! I know without a doubt that living out your God-ordained purpose and doing it well is all that matters.

The Philanthropist: My organizations, *"**GirlFight** ™ – The Conflict Resolution Solution"* and *"**Charming ME** ™ – Cultivating Class with Christ"*, are just two ways in which I sow back into the world. Both of these programs are designed to grow and mentor girls and young woman to become positive thinkers, peacekeepers, and poised, purposed women – with low, to no cost involved.

I am M.E. Porter – The Soul Shifter.

Dedicated mother of three beautiful daughters.

The Transformational trailblazer.

Divinely equipped with the wisdom and compassion to facilitate

change in all arenas; personal, spiritual, and business.

I am dancing through life filled with passion to provoke all that it

takes to bring about a shift in the lives of all whom I encounter.

When all is well in my Soul; all is well in the world.

Book M.E. for:

Keynote, Session or Breakout Speaker.

Panelist, Host, Retreat Facilitator.

Spiritual Advising, Coaching or Mentoring events.

Office: (404) 500-8722

Contact Email: info@marilyneporter.com

Website: www.marilyneporter.com or www.motivationallyme.com

Facebook: http://www.fb.com/IamMEPorter

Twitter: http://www.twitter.com/MEMotivates

Email your reviews of this book to the email address provided above.

4

THE PIECES

OF

YOU

When all is well in my Soul; all is well in the world.

DOING THE WORK

14 What good is it, my brothers and sisters, if you say you have faith but do not have works? Can faith save you? 15 If a brother or sister is naked and lacks daily food, 16 and one of you says to them, "Go in peace; keep warm and eat your fill," and yet you do not supply their bodily needs, what is the good of that? 17 So faith by itself, if it has no works, is dead. **James 2:14-17 NIV**

Write a letter to yourself as a child that expresses the love, kindness and compassion that you now know you deserved. Explain to your child-self why it is important to forgive those who may have hurt you and share with your child-self how valuable each of your life experiences has been.

Date _____

Dear _____,

_____
_____
_____
_____
_____
_____
_____
_____
_____
_____
_____

When all is well in my Soul; all is well in the world.

The Pieces of ME

When all is well in my Soul; all is well in the world.

Write a letter to your future-self (10 or 15 years from today). Express to your future-self how proud you are of how far you have come on the journey. Give your future-self all of the love and admiration that she deserves for staying the course and not giving up when things were tough. Reveal the success of your dreams and goals in this letter to your future-self.

Date _____

Dear _____,

_____
_____
_____
_____
_____
_____
_____
_____
_____

When all is well in my Soul; all is well in the world.

The Pieces of ME

Write a letter to your PRESENT-self. Remind yourself that the present is a gift and where you are right now matters. Be honest with where you are in this moment. Tell yourself the truth about who you are today. Then EMRACE IT!

Date_____

Dear _____,

_____
_____
_____
_____
_____
_____
_____
_____
_____
_____
_____
_____
_____

When all is well in my Soul; all is well in the world.

The Pieces of ME

What are your 5 greatest strengths?

1. _____
2. _____
3. _____
4. _____
5. _____

CELEBRATE THEM!

What are your five greatest weaknesses?

1. _____
2. _____
3. _____
4. _____
5. _____

IMPROVE THEM!

When all is well in my Soul; all is well in the world.

One of my most powerful daily affirmations comes from The Bible – the Scripture comes from Ephesians 2:10, *"For we are His **workmanship**, created in Christ Jesus unto good works, which God hath before ordained that we should walk in them."* From this passage of scripture, I focused on the word "workmanship". This word translates from the original Greek to the word *"poiema"*, which is where we get the English word *poem*. Although the passage is not actually calling us God's poems, it is more accurately referring to us as *works of art* (for the purposes of this assignment, I have coined **The Ephesians 210 Project** ™, and we will use the word *poem*).

My daily affirmation: "God wrote a love poem, and He titled it *Marilyn Elizabeth*".

Your assignment is to write a poem from the heart of God that describes YOU. So turn the page and begin writing!

(The title of YOUR poem)

When all is well in my Soul; all is well in the world.

The Pieces of ME

THE PIECE OF YOU

Tell ME Your:

Dreams

_____
_____
_____
_____
_____
_____
_____
_____
_____
_____
_____
_____
_____
_____

My Dream is to leave a legacy of faith, integrity and wealth.

When all is well in my Soul; all is well in the world.

The Pieces of ME

Ideas

_____

_____

_____

_____

_____

_____

_____

_____

_____

_____

_____

_____

_____

_____

My ideas are to define love, freedom, faith and self-awareness.

Goals

My goals are to achieve the very best of ME in all things.

When all is well in my Soul; all is well in the world.

The Pieces of ME

Fears

_____
_____
_____
_____
_____
_____
_____
_____
_____
_____
_____
_____
_____
_____
_____
_____

My fears are not being loved and disappointing my children.

What events have shaped your life?

Hearing my father say he didn't love ME shaped my life.

When all is well in my Soul; all is well in the world.

The Pieces of ME

What do you need to do better for yourself?

_____

_____

_____

_____

_____

_____

_____

_____

_____

_____

_____

_____

_____

_____

_____

I need to eat healthier and rest more for myself.

What gifts do you owe The World that you have not shared?

_____

_____

_____

_____

_____

_____

_____

_____

_____

_____

_____

_____

_____

_____

_____

_____

_____

_____

I am sharing all of my gifts with The World!

When all is well in my Soul; all is well in the world.

The Pieces of ME

Who do you need to forgive?

_____
_____
_____
_____
_____
_____
_____
_____
_____
_____
_____
_____
_____
_____
_____
_____
_____
_____

I have forgiven all; including ME.

When all is well in my Soul; all is well in the world.

The Pieces of ME

How are you serving others?

I am serving others through ministry and mentoring.

When all is well in my Soul; all is well in the world.

The Pieces of ME

AFFIRM ME

TO LIFE!

(AND YOU)

When all is well in my Soul; all is well in the world.

My Success Does NOT Require Your Validation But I Appreciate Your Support

www.marilyneporter.com

I am a creation of

The Divine Creator.

My mind is strong.

My heart is open.

My body is healthy.

My Spirit is willing.

I am a child of God

M.E. Porter

21 Ways to Soul-Filled Living

1. Tell yourself the truth – not your truth but THE truth.

2. Accept the truth.

3. Rest in the truth.

4. Release the lie and accept that it was a lie.

5. Embrace every component of who you are.

6. Embrace the worst of you.

7. Embrace your flaws.

8. Embrace your weaknesses.

9. Accept that YOU are perfectly imperfect.

10. Celebrate the best of you.

When all is well in my Soul; all is well in the world.

21 Ways...

11. Celebrate the things you absolutely admire about you.

12. Celebrate your strengths.

13. Celebrate your power.

14. Stand in ALL of you boldly.

15. Give thanks for ALL of you.

16. Smile at your reflection.

17. Give yourself the gift of silence every day.

18. Give love freely.

19. Forgive yourself and others quickly.

20. Have faith.

21. Be kind to your instincts; listen to your soul.

Use "_21 Ways to Soul-Filled Living_"

To create your own set of Soul-filled daily affirmations.

1. _____

2. _____

3. _____

4. _____

5. _____

6. _____

7. _____

8. _____

When all is well in my Soul; all is well in the world.

Beloved, if you have done the work within the pages of this book, then you are ready to begin the journey of bringing your own broken, shattered, and fallen pieces together. Healing starts *now*!

CHAPTER ONE

The

Pieces of

YOU

When all is well in my Soul; all is well in the world.

The Pieces of YOU

The Pieces of YOU

When all is well in my Soul; all is well in the world.

The Pieces of YOU

The Pieces of YOU

When all is well in my Soul; all is well in the world.

The Pieces of YOU

The Pieces of YOU

When all is well in my Soul; all is well in the world.

The Pieces of YOU

The Pieces of YOU

When all is well in my Soul; all is well in the world.

The Pieces of YOU

The Pieces of YOU

When all is well in my Soul; all is well in the world.

The Pieces of YOU

The Pieces of YOU

When all is well in my Soul; all is well in the world.

The Pieces of YOU

The Pieces of YOU

When all is well in my Soul; all is well in the world.

The Pieces of YOU

The Pieces of YOU

When all is well in my Soul; all is well in the world.

The Pieces of YOU

The Pieces of YOU

When all is well in my Soul; all is well in the world.

The Pieces of YOU

The Pieces of YOU

When all is well in my Soul; all is well in the world.

The Pieces of YOU

The Pieces of YOU

When all is well in my Soul; all is well in the world.

The Pieces of YOU

The Pieces of YOU

When all is well in my Soul; all is well in the world.

The Pieces of YOU

The Pieces of YOU

When all is well in my Soul; all is well in the world.

The Pieces of YOU

The Pieces of YOU

When all is well in my Soul; all is well in the world.

AND NOW THIS BOOK CONTAINS

"THE PIECES OF YOU"

AND

ME

I bid you blessings, love, and unmerited favor.

Enjoy the journey!

M.E.

When all is well in my Soul; all is well in the world.

www.ingramcontent.com/pod-product-compliance
Lightning Source LLC
Chambersburg PA
CBHW071630080526
44588CB00010B/1340